WORLD *of* WONDER

the DEEP BLUE

Charlotte Guillain

Lou Baker Smith

For Rachel - C.G.

For my family. You are my sun, my
moon, my ocean, and all of my stars. - L.B.S.

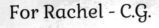

Quarto is the authority on a wide range of topics.

Quarto educates, entertains and enriches the lives of
our readers—enthusiasts and lovers of hands-on living.

www.quartoknows.com

Consultant: Michael Bright
Art Director: Susi Martin
Editor: Harriet Stone
Creative Director: Malena Stojic
Publisher: Rhiannon Findlay

© 2020 Quarto Publishing plc
Text © 2020 Charlotte Guillain
Illustration © 2020 Lou Baker Smith

Charlotte Guillain has asserted her right to be identified as the author of this work.
Lou Baker Smith has asserted her right to be identified as the illustrator of this work.

This edition first published in 2020 by words & pictures,
an imprint of The Quarto Group.
26391 Crown Valley Parkway, Suite 220
Mission Viejo, CA 92691, USA
T: +1 949 380 7510
F: +1 949 380 7575
www.QuartoKnows.com

A CIP record for this book is available from the Library of Congress.

ISBN 978 0 7112 5010 9

Manufactured in Guangdong, China EB012021

9 8 7 6 5 4 3 2 1

Contents

World of Water

Seen from space, Earth is a ball of blue. The oceans make up over 70 percent of our planet's surface, from the vast Pacific to the smallest seas. The crashing waves, dark depths, and still, turquoise waters of our oceans are all home to a multitude of life. Much of the ocean is yet to be discovered and explored by humans.

The world's oceans are one immense, connected body of water. Although there are five distinct oceans—the Pacific, Atlantic, Indian, Southern, and Arctic—they are interlinked, with currents flowing through them all. These currents create our weather and bring life to the seas by carrying food and warmth around the globe. Some currents move only in the surface waters but others travel in the deepest reaches of the sea.

The Pacific is the largest and deepest ocean, bigger than all the continents and almost all the other oceans put together. Its name means "peaceful" but the waters of the Pacific can rise up to swell and crash in terrifying storms.

Life on our planet depends on the oceans. More than half of the oxygen we need to live is produced by plants in our seas. This world of water is full of wonders but is also vital for all living things on Earth.

The Pull of the Tide

Water laps and creeps up the beach under a moonlit sky. Soon the shore has vanished underwater, as waves roll steadily onto the land. By daybreak, the sea has slipped away again, leaving shining pebbles and gleaming mudflats to dry in the morning sun. In and out, in and out—the tides are constantly moving.

Moved by the Moon, the water in Earth's oceans is pulled to make tides. The Moon's gravity drags the sea so it bulges out at high tide, moving the water toward the coastline. As Earth spins, parts of the ocean move away from the Moon's pull and there is a low tide. This happens twice a day.

When the tide goes out, parts of the seabed that are normally covered by the ocean are revealed. Tiny creatures are left in shallow pools until the waters crawl back up the beach. In and out, in and out—the tides are the rhythmic heartbeat of the ocean.

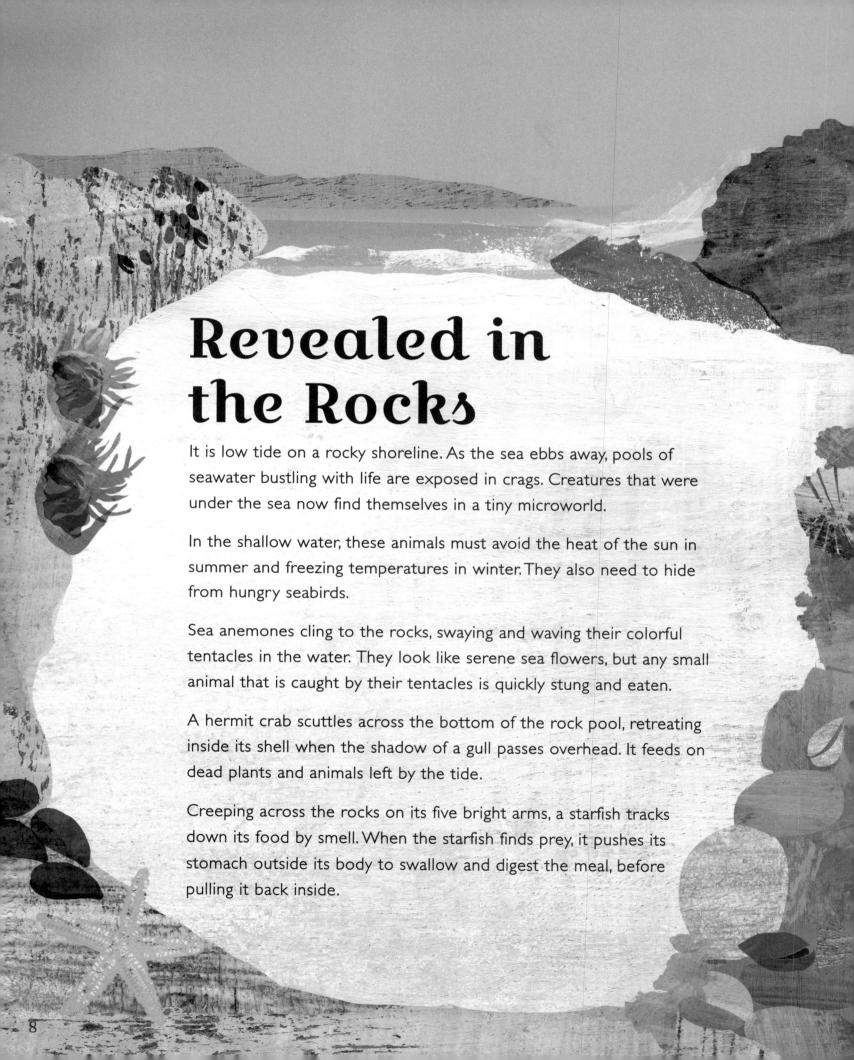

Revealed in the Rocks

It is low tide on a rocky shoreline. As the sea ebbs away, pools of seawater bustling with life are exposed in crags. Creatures that were under the sea now find themselves in a tiny microworld.

In the shallow water, these animals must avoid the heat of the sun in summer and freezing temperatures in winter. They also need to hide from hungry seabirds.

Sea anemones cling to the rocks, swaying and waving their colorful tentacles in the water. They look like serene sea flowers, but any small animal that is caught by their tentacles is quickly stung and eaten.

A hermit crab scuttles across the bottom of the rock pool, retreating inside its shell when the shadow of a gull passes overhead. It feeds on dead plants and animals left by the tide.

Creeping across the rocks on its five bright arms, a starfish tracks down its food by smell. When the starfish finds prey, it pushes its stomach outside its body to swallow and digest the meal, before pulling it back inside.

Gradually, the faint crash of the distant waves
becomes louder as the tide starts to rise.
Soon the pool will be submerged once more.

Crashing Waves

Waves swoop up and crash against the shoreline, the surf spraying up in a salty mist. The swooshing rumble repeats. Waves begin far out at sea, where wind whips across the water. The wind's energy moves across the surface of the sea, spinning and pushing the water up and down. This movement begins as a ripple and builds up into a wave that swells and swirls onward toward the coast. As the ocean becomes shallow near the shore, the waves curl up and then crash and roar as surf, carving out the coastline as they thunder and break onto the beach.

Where the River Meets the Sea

Off the coast of Brazil, the Atlantic Ocean is stained brown. The colossal Amazon River empties into the ocean here, bringing tons of mud with it. The river's fresh water floats above the salty sea water, the brown, muddy cloud stretching for over 300,000 square miles (1 million sq km). One sixth of the planet's fresh water is emptied into the Atlantic from the Amazon.

As well as the muddy sediment, the river water carries plant matter and other nutrients from upstream. This rich mixture provides food for many living things in the ocean. Under the murky river water on the surface, plankton blooms in the sea. On the seabed there is a reef of rocklike algae, home to many fish, huge sponges, and other sea creatures.

A Swirling Shoal

Deep below the surface, currents are carrying tiny food particles through the ocean. When the wind blows along the shore, the current streams toward the surface, bringing nutrients to feed microscopic plankton in the water. As the plankton spread, fish gather to feast on them. A shoal of shiny sardines sweeps and swooshes through the surface water as they feed, but the sardines are not the only hungry creatures in this part of the ocean.

Soon larger fish, dolphins, and sharks appear, making the sardines gather into a huge swirling ball. The sea churns as the shimmering sardines spin in the sunlit waters. Inside the dense sphere, most sardines are able to hide from the predators and confuse them with their spiraling movements. But the sardines are surrounded. Sea birds dive into the water and pick them off from above, while ocean hunters work together to attack the fish from all sides. How long can the swirling shoal survive?

Underwater Forest

An enormous forest of fronds grows in the cool, shallow water off the coast of Canada. Vast, green-brown towers reach up from the ocean floor and spread out at the sunlit surface.
They are giant kelp, a kind of super-sized seaweed. This amazing algae can grow to be over 100 feet (30 m) tall. Kelp can grow fast in cold, coastal waters, sometimes as much as 18 inches (45 cm) a day. Forests of kelp cover a quarter of the world's shoreline.

Down on the seabed, the bottom of each seaweed clings to rocks, using a rootlike holdfast. These sprawling anchors are hideaway homes for small creatures, such as worms, snails, and brittlestars. Fish also lay their eggs there, away from hungry predators.

A flexible, stemlike stipe stretches upward from
each holdfast. They sway to the rhythm of the
tides and the current, the whole forest dancing to
the movement of the ocean. Shoals of fish dart
and hide among the waving weeds, while larger
animals, such as sea lions, shelter among the kelp
during storms.

At the surface, kelp fronds spread out and
bob, their gas-filled blades keeping them afloat.
The slimy kelp spreads in mats for miles at the
top of shallow water to absorb energy from
the sun's rays and keep the forest fed.

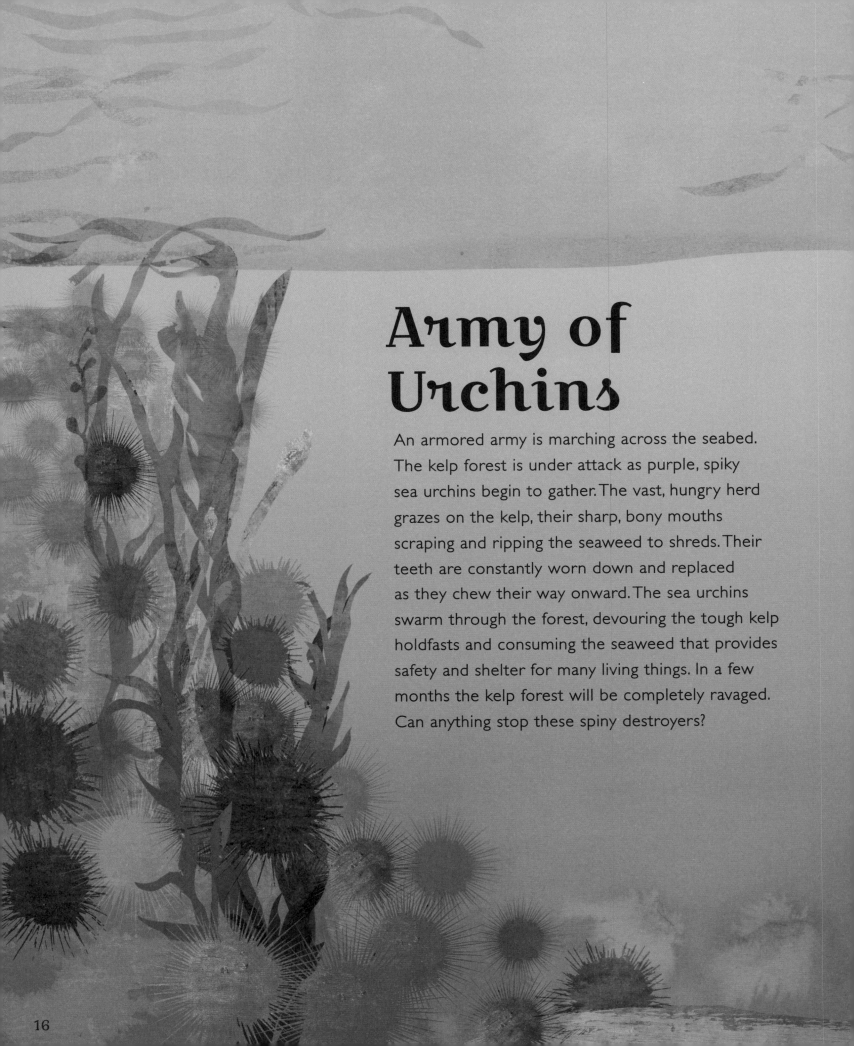

Army of Urchins

An armored army is marching across the seabed. The kelp forest is under attack as purple, spiky sea urchins begin to gather. The vast, hungry herd grazes on the kelp, their sharp, bony mouths scraping and ripping the seaweed to shreds. Their teeth are constantly worn down and replaced as they chew their way onward. The sea urchins swarm through the forest, devouring the tough kelp holdfasts and consuming the seaweed that provides safety and shelter for many living things. In a few months the kelp forest will be completely ravaged. Can anything stop these spiny destroyers?

Forest Guardian

Wrapped in strands of slippery kelp, a sea otter dozes in the warm sun. His thick fur absorbs the heat as he sleeps. But another sea otter is ready to eat. Splash! She dives to the bottom of the kelp strands, spotting her prickly prey as her streamlined body shoots downward. She grabs a sea urchin and a rock from the sea bed and speeds back to the surface. Now she floats on her back, holding the rock on her stomach. Bash! She hits the urchin against the rock to break it open before eating it. Kelp forests give the otters a safe place to live and they in turn stop the urchins from destroying their seaweed home.

Trees in the Ocean

In the warmer waters of tropical coastlines, such as around Indonesia, trees rise out of the sea. Magical mangrove forests fringe the shores for hundreds of thousands of miles, their roots submerged in sea water when the tide is high.

How do the mangroves survive in salty water? These tough, tangled trees can remove the salt from their system through their leaves or else block it from entering their roots in the first place.

The mangroves' sprawling roots twist and curve above the seabed. When the tide is high, these roots provide a safe place for young fish and other creatures to feed and hide from predators while they grow.

The twisting, intertwined root systems also help to hold the coastline together, stopping the tide from dragging soil away from the shore. When a storm hits or high waves crash, the mangrove barrier slows the movement of water and helps to stop the land from being worn away.

A mangrove's seeds begin to grow while they are still on their parent tree. When the time is right, they drop into the ocean and float away, until they settle on a new shoreline. Then they will put down roots of their own and another mangrove forest will start to grow.

Graceful Grazers

A mother and her calf move lazily among the mangroves off the coast of Florida, USA. Their bulky bodies swim slowly and gracefully through the warm, shallow water as the mother searches for plants to eat. These gentle, gray creatures are manatees. Every few minutes they push the tips of their noses out of the water to breathe before silently sinking down once more.

When the tide is high, the mangroves provide a haven of food for the mother, whose baby is still feeding on her milk. She flaps her fan-shaped tail and pulls herself along the seabed using her flippers, searching this sheltered shoreline for her next meal. The manatee grazes on algae, weeds, and sea grass growing in watery meadows near the mangrove roots. She pulls herself out of the water to nibble the mangrove leaves. The manatee feeds for up to eight hours a day and then rests in the shelter of the mangroves, keeping her calf close by.

A Marine Meadow

A green meadow sweeps across the seabed in shallow, turquoise waters near the Australian coast. This carpet of seagrass provides food and shelter for a throng of living things. Seagrass is not a seaweed, like kelp. This plant has roots, stems, and leaves and even produces flowers. It grows in warm surface waters so it can bask in the sunlight it uses to make energy and oxygen. This ocean grassland works hard to keep the sea healthy—where seagrass grows, the water is cleaner. A seagrass meadow can also absorb and store 35 times as much carbon dioxide as an area of rainforest the same size.

Turtle Grass

The green sea turtle travels enormous distances as it migrates across the ocean. The seagrass meadow is a welcome sanctuary on its journey, providing a feast of plants in the shallow waters. When the tide is low, it is safe for the turtle to graze, sometimes eating over 4 pounds (2 kg) of grass a day. It slices through the tips of the blades easily with its sawlike mouth. This trimming of the plant's stems helps them to grow, but when the tide turns and the water becomes deeper, the turtle must look out for sharks and other predators. It is time for the turtle to move on.

The Incredible Coral Polyp

Not far from the Caribbean shore, in a warm, shallow ocean, a strange animal is feeding. This curious little creature is a coral polyp. It floated to this place as a minuscule larva, and now that it is fully grown it will never move again. The soft polyp built itself a hard skeleton, using natural chemicals it took in from the seawater. The polyp has chosen to make its home in this sunlit, clear part of the ocean so it can feed. As the sun's rays warm the water, colorful, microscopic algae living inside the polyp use the sunlight to make food. But why do the polyp's bright tentacles wave in the water? At night, when there is no sunlight, it stretches out its swaying, venomous arms to grab plankton in the water to eat. A single coral polyp can divide and reproduce itself thousands of times, building up an enormous, spectacular reef.

A Teeming Reef

Off the coast of northeast Australia, a living wonder stretches for over 1,240 miles (2,000 km). An immense stretch of coral reefs and islands makes up the Great Barrier Reef, the largest living structure on Earth. Thousands of different species make their home in the vibrant world of the colorful coral.

Shoals of tiny, brightly colored fish dart through the sun-dappled water. Dazzling royal angelfish nibble the coral. They shoot off to find a hiding place as soon as a shark's shadow appears overhead.

A striped, orange clownfish seeks safety in the stinging tentacles of an anemone. Slime on the clownfish's body protects it from the anemone's toxic sting. Predators won't dare to come near the fish here.

A tiny seahorse bobs through the shallow water, propelled by its delicate, fluttering fin. It uses its curled tail to grip the coral and anchor itself safely in the reef.

Something is squeezing out of a crevice deep in the reef. A blue-ringed octopus is on the hunt. It is camouflaged while it lies in wait for prey, but if it is threatened, it will turn bright yellow with flashing blue rings. This mesmerizing octopus is one of the most venomous creatures in the ocean.

Blue Lagoon

In the warm waters of the Indian Ocean, a ring-shaped reef hides behind the crash and swell of the high waves. This is an atoll reef, fringed by aquamarine sea and with a deep blue lagoon in its center. The atoll began to form when an undersea volcano erupted long ago. Lava piled up on the ocean floor, building to form an isolated island called a seamount. Over time, coral polyps settled around the top of the island in the sunlit surface water and spread to create a circular reef. Then, over millions of years, the seamount sank back below the waves and created a calm lagoon in the middle of the reef. The atoll and the sheltered lagoon are home to many fish and other sea creatures. Dolphins, turtles, rays, and sharks all visit this ocean oasis to feed and rest.

Reef Guard

The coral is not safe. A band of crown-of-thorns starfish is ransacking a reef in the southern Pacific Ocean. They are devouring the coral and leaving devastation in their wake. What can stop these poisonous predators, with their vicious spines and enormous appetite? Luckily the reef has a determined defender. The tiny, red-speckled coral guard-crab makes its home on the reef, where it can feed, safe from predators. The crab will fight to preserve its habitat. When hordes of starfish threaten its sanctuary, the crimson crab pinches and nips at their tubelike feet, sending them away. This snappy sentinel also uses its claws to stop coral-eating snails from damaging its home.

A Bleached Reef

The ocean's reefs face a much more terrible threat.
Earth's climate is heating up and so the water in the
sea is warming. When the temperature of the ocean
around a reef rises too high, the algae that live in
each polyp leave the coral. The algae give the coral
its bright colors and supply it with food. With the
algae gone, the coral can no longer get its food from
the sunlight and it turns pale. The reef becomes
bleached, with life leeching away. The bare bones of
the once bustling paradise now stand still and stark
on the ocean floor.

The Open Ocean

The undulating blue of the open ocean stretches to the horizon in all directions. No land or life is visible, just the rise and fall of the rolling waves. This enormous expanse of water, also known as the pelagic zone, covers over half of the Earth's surface.

Sunlight sparkles on the water and the only sound is the wind, whipping up spray. But now a shadow is looming up from the depths. A strange, deep call vibrates below the surface. A long, tapered shape slips through the water, then a colossal blue whale surges up to the surface of the ocean. The largest creature on the planet bursts from the blue, raising its flippers and twisting in the air. The blue whale crashes back down into the water with a gargantuan splash! Coming back up for air, this marine giant arcs its way gracefully through the sea, shooting spray high into the sky from its blowhole.

Suddenly, the blue whale dives, tilting its wide tail up above the waves before disappearing. It glides back down to deeper waters, only coming back to the surface to feed on krill and breathe. For now, the open ocean is quiet once more.

Storm Swell

A storm is stirring in the skies above the open ocean. The once calm, warm waters are thrashing and crashing as huge, lowering clouds gather overhead. Hot, wet air has risen from the ocean's surface and now cool, dry air is moving in to replace it. The air spins and swirls as winds whip across the waves, causing massive swells up to 100 feet (30 m) high. Now a hurricane hurtles across the ocean, twisting and whirling as the dark sea surges and thundering rain pummels the surface. The wind howls. The ocean churns. But at last, the tropical cyclone roars on toward land, leaving the open ocean to settle and calm as the sun breaks through the clouds.

A Sea Swallow

Far from land, above the Southern Ocean, a little bird is making its long journey from the Arctic to Antarctica. The Arctic tern has been traveling for two months, diving down and dipping its beak into the sea to feed on fish as it flies. The tiny tern is so light, it can glide on the wind, even sleeping as it travels on over the ocean. This black-capped "sea swallow" is following the summer from the northern to the southern hemisphere, where the seasons are opposite. It heads to Antarctica for its long days of summer sunlight before flying back to the Arctic in spring to breed and feed.

A Bloom in the Ocean

Clouds of green are swirling through the blue of the open ocean. Phytoplankton are blooming and filling the surface waters. These are the tiny plants that so much other life in the ocean food web depends on.

Microscopic phytoplankton includes a huge amount of simple plants called algae. They float in the light-filled water at the surface of the ocean to soak up the sun's rays and create energy. Like land plants, they produce oxygen and store carbon dioxide, much of which falls to the bottom of the ocean.

When the right amount of sunlight shines on the sea and currents bring up nutrients from deeper waters, the phytoplankton flourish. And where the phytoplankton blooms, other life thrives. Tiny, shrimplike creatures, such as krill, devour the clouds of algae. They in turn attract huge, hungry shoals of small fish, which are then eaten by larger predators. Sharks, dolphins, and whales all come to join the feast.

When night falls, millions of minuscule stars seem to glow in the blackness of the ocean. Chemicals in the phytoplankton react to produce bioluminescent light that shimmers on the dark surf. These tiny dots of algae have filled the sea with life and light.

Stinging Swarm

Out in the open ocean, a throng of stinging creatures is being carried by the current. Delicate, jelly-like blobs bob and sway in the sea with long tentacles streaming below them. This bloom of jellyfish may grow to cover several square miles, following the clouds of plankton that are spreading through the water.

Translucent, soft jellyfish can be brightly colored or almost see-through. When night falls and the ocean becomes a vast expanse of darkness, some jellyfish light up. Their bioluminescent bodies swoosh through the black water like strange glowing aliens.

Jellyfish have been drifting around our oceans for millions of years, feeding on tiny sea life. They can quickly grow or shrink in size, depending on how much food is around them. They stay close together so they can easily reproduce.

Boneless, bloodless, brainless jellyfish are mostly made of water. They squeeze their rubbery, dome-shaped bodies to push themselves through the sea, their stinging tentacles trailing behind them. These dangling stingers entangle and paralyze prey with poison as the jellyfish passes by. The jellyfish then opens the mouth in the middle of its body and digests its meal, before pushing out any waste.

Now the alien swarm moves on with the current, swishing and bobbing away.

Plastic Ocean

There is another great swarm floating in the open ocean. What creatures have come together to build up this enormous mass of color? Is this gathering made up of plants or animals? Neither. This is the Great Pacific Garbage Patch, a colossal area of the ocean covered in plastic rubbish. Millions of tons of plastic are floating throughout the oceans, but currents bring great patches of it together, where

it drifts in a deadly slick. Seabirds get tangled in plastic and can't fly. Turtles mistake floating plastic bags for jellyfish and swallow them. Whales' stomachs fill with plastic. It could be hundreds of years before the plastic is worn away by the sun and broken up into minuscule particles. Even then those tiny pieces will stay floating in the ocean, becoming part of the food chain and harming many creatures. In an ocean full of life, the sea of plastic does not belong.

The Deep Ocean

Travel down from the sunlit surface waters and enter the dim, chill world of the deep ocean. There are no plants down here, away from the sunlight that they need to make energy. Any plant-eating animals living in the deep ocean can only feed on particles that drop down from the upper reaches of the sea. Life is very different in the cold and murky world of the depths.

Just 660 feet (200 m) below the surface, the twilight zone begins. Only the faintest light can be detected here. Travel farther down and the midnight zone starts 3,300 feet (1,000 m) from the ocean's surface. Here the sea is as dark as the blackest night.

On the ocean floor, the water temperature is intensely cold and the pressure created by all the water above is immense. It seems impossible that anything could survive in the darkest, deepest reaches of the ocean. And yet the deep sea is the largest habitat on the planet, home to a wealth of life. Strange creatures that have adapted to extremes thrive in places that humans have barely explored.

The Twilight Zone

Strange creatures lurk in the murky waters of the twilight zone, 660 feet (200 m) down. The sun's light barely penetrates this deep into the ocean, so how do the inhabitants of this shadowy world find food? For many, the answer is to make their own light. The lanternfish creates blue-green bioluminescence in its body through a chemical reaction. The fish's eerie glow lures in smaller fish, which quickly become its next meal.

Other creatures produce a startling flash of colored light to frighten predators away.
For some, producing dots of light helps to break up the outline of their bodies, confusing
hungry hunters. Glowing in the darkness is also one of the only ways these deep-sea
dwellers can attract a mate and reproduce. There may be more life in the gloomy twilight
zone than anywhere else in the ocean, and almost all the creatures here glitter with light.

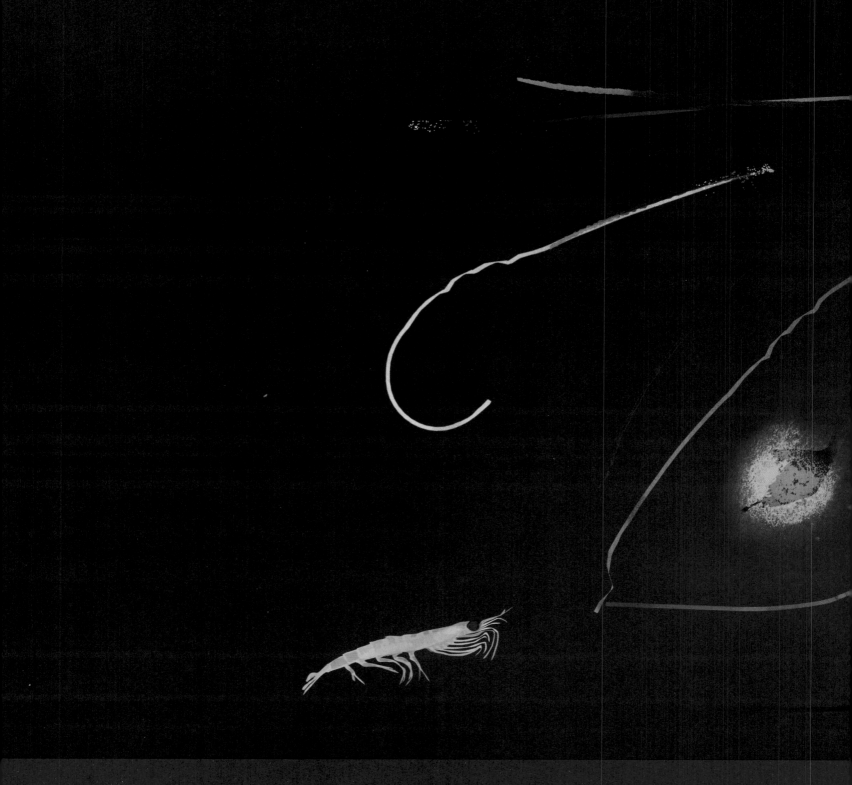

The Midnight Zone

The midnight zone…a world of sheer blackness where the temperature is just above freezing. Yet fish, jellyfish, mollusks, and crustaceans all survive in this chilling darkness. A terrifying creature looms out of the black expanse. A hairy anglerfish is on the hunt. Her wide gaping jaws, full of jagged, spiny teeth, hang menacingly open. Long, hairlike antennae float out from her deep red body, feeling for movement from any unsuspecting prey.

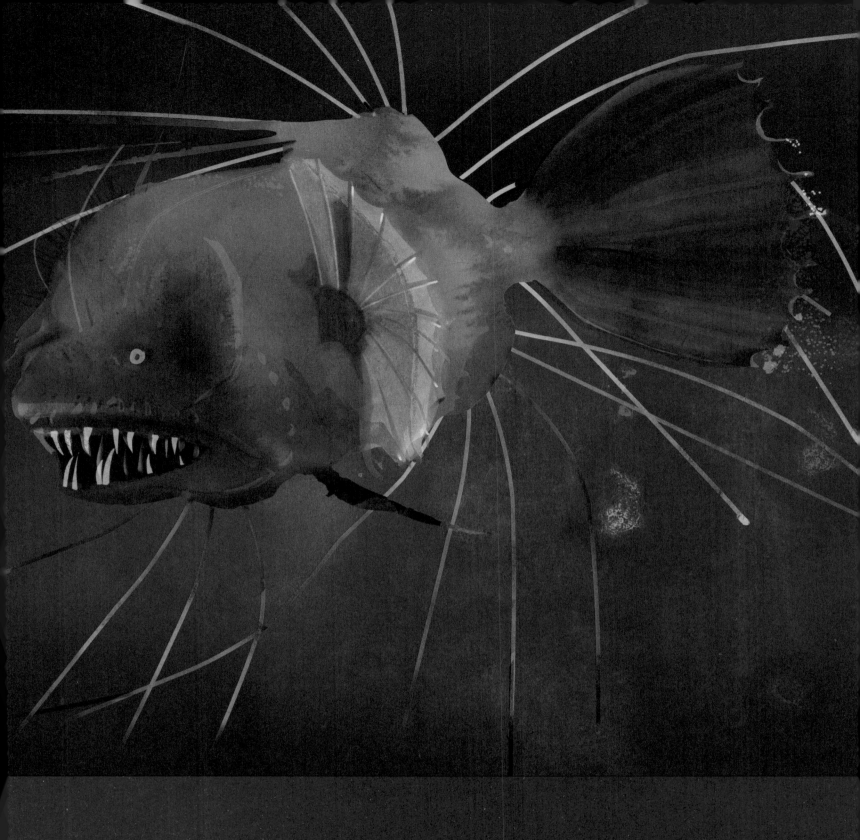

Her two huge, unblinking eyes stare out into the gloom that is lit only by the glowing lure that extends from her head like a fishing rod. Now a shrimp swims toward the blob of light that she twitches in the darkness. Is it food? The hairy anglerfish strikes when she feels her prey is close. Her stomach can expand to make room for a large meal, giving her the energy she needs until it is time to lie in wait in the blackness again.

Deepwater Chimneys

Tall chimneys reach up from the floor of the
Pacific Ocean, spewing out super-heated clouds.
These hydrothermal vents are a haven of life
in the cold and darkness of the deep.

The volcanic vents are underwater hot springs that
were created by melted rock under the ocean floor.
Water filtered through cracks in the volcanic rock
at the bottom of the sea and was heated by the
molten magma below. The water then gushed back
upward, carrying dissolved particles of minerals
with it. These minerals hardened in the cool
water above and piled up into tall towers.

The plumes of fluid gushing out of the top of the vents can be as hot as 750°F (400°C), but are instantly cooled by the freezing deep-ocean water. The vents also release natural chemicals that feed microscopic bacteria, which in turn provide food for the hundreds of species that can live in the intense heat around the chimneys. Bright red worms living in tubes attached to the vents get their energy from the bacteria, as do shrimp, crabs, fish, mussels, and many other creatures. An abundance of life has adapted to live in this extreme part of the ocean.

Into the Abyss

Around 2.5 miles (4 km) down, the ocean
falls away into the depths of the abyss.
The ocean floor up to this point has been
part of the continental shelf—the ground
that slopes down under the ocean from
the edges of Earth's continents. But this
far down, the sea bed drops away until
it becomes the abyssal plain. Down here,
the ocean floor is flat and the water is
so cold it's almost at the freezing point.
Very little life is found, apart from a
few boneless creatures such as squid or
starfish. The mud on the seabed can be
over a mile (1.6 km) thick. Deep trenches
run for hundreds of miles, gouging
out gashes across the ocean floor.
The Mariana Trench in the Pacific Ocean
is the deepest, falling away to depths of
over 6.8 miles (11 km). Who knows what
secrets this underwater world holds?

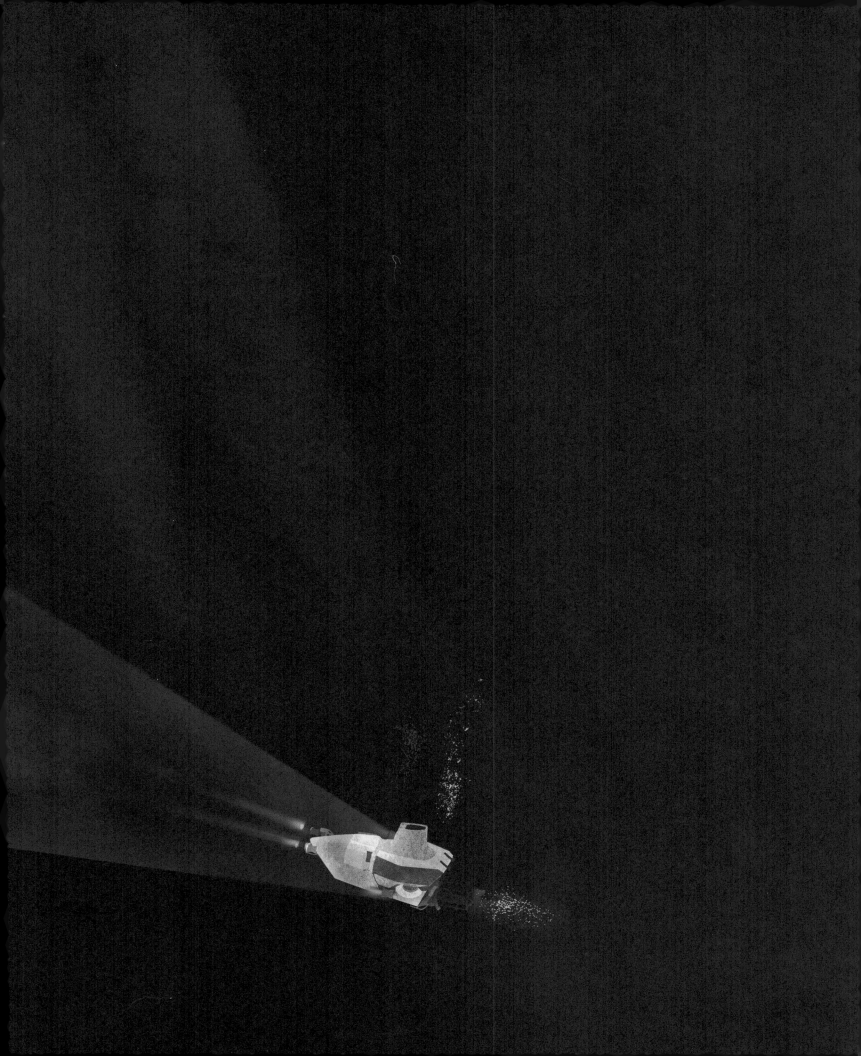

Deep-sea Mountains

In the middle of the abyssal plain, ridges of rock rise up from the ocean floor. These underwater mountains run for thousands of miles across the seabed, making them the longest mountain ranges on the planet. These mid-ocean ridges formed where two huge plates of rock floating on the Earth's mantle lie alongside each other. The mantle is a layer of magma that lies beneath the Earth's surface. Where two plates of rock on the mantle meet, they can push against each other or pull apart. When a gap appears, molten magma gushes up from the mantle, raising the rock on the ocean floor. This has created ridges and valleys, including some massive mountain ranges that rise 2 miles (3.2 km) from the seabed.

Extreme Eruption

There is fire at the bottom of the Pacific Ocean. An underwater volcano is erupting where two plates of rock jostle against each other. Red-hot lava is spewing out through cracks in the seabed and exploding into the cold sea water. The water pressure this deep is enormous, pushing down on the lava as soon as it emerges into the ocean. The fiery lava oozes out, folding over itself as it solidifies into smooth, dark, glassy shapes. When it meets the freezing ocean water, clouds of steam form so quickly that they can shatter the rock around them. Over thousands of years, the eruptions have built up into piles of volcanic rock, called seamounts. Most of the volcanic eruptions on the planet happen

The Frozen Ocean

Far away from fiery lava, the frozen ocean is a world of ice. Huge, blue-white giants float in the freezing water. These icebergs drift in the Arctic and Southern Oceans, sitting on the surface of the polar seas. These vast frozen crags are huge chunks of freshwater ice that broke away from the coastline. Icebergs creak and crash as they split away from a glacier and float away, carried by the wind and the ocean's currents. The bulk of an iceberg is hidden beneath the water, with just the tip visible above the surface. In the warm summer months these hulking ice chunks float freely. They can tip over and flip without warning as they melt, sending huge waves across the water around them. In winter the icebergs become still, frozen into the sea ice around them.

Incredible Krill

A mass of creatures is gathering in the Southern Ocean. Tiny, pink, shrimplike krill crowd in clouds under the ice in the largest gathering of any species on the planet. Their swirling swarms can turn the surface of the sea a reddish-pink.

The krill have large black eyes and translucent bodies with many legs. In the blackness of night, they can glow with bioluminescence, lighting up the freezing ocean. Krill swim down to the depths of the sea during the day but migrate to the surface at night to feed. Away from the safety of the deeper water, they must try to avoid hordes of hungry predators that are also looking for a meal.

Krill are eaten by a range of sea creatures, from fish, penguins, and seals all the way up to the largest animal on Earth, the blue whale. Each of these animals can eat thousands of krill at a time.

When the surface of the ocean is frozen
in winter, the krill survive by nibbling the
algae that grows on the underside of the
ice. They can shrink to a smaller size to save
energy during these dark winter months. In
spring, the ice starts to melt and sunlight
penetrates the surface water again. Now
phytoplankton can grow in large blooms,
providing a feast for the krill, which once
more swarm in their millions.

The Unicorn of the Sea

The unicorn of the sea is emerging through the ice in the Arctic Ocean, raising a sword to the sky. The narwhal is a toothed whale, with a spiral, spearlike tusk that extends from the male's upper jaw. This tusk is an extra-long tooth that can sense changes and movement in the icy ocean. Narwhals spend the winter under the Arctic sea ice, hunting in groups and feeding on fish, shrimp, and squid. Like all mammals, they need to breathe air, so they pop up through cracks in the ice to take a breath before diving down deep to feed again.

Antifreeze Fish

In the sub-zero waters of the Southern Ocean, how do fish avoid freezing in the extreme temperatures? Icefish have an amazing solution. Some fish, such as sailfin plunderfish, have adapted to produce special antifreeze proteins that stop ice crystals from growing and spreading in their bodies. These proteins attach themselves to ice crystals that form inside the fish in extreme temperatures and stop them from damaging the fish's body. Antarctic silverfish lay eggs that float up to the surface and lie under the ice. Here, they are safe from most predators and are kept at a sheltered temperature where the young fish can develop.

Melting Sea Ice

At the planet's poles, the oceans freeze in winter. When the sun disappears for months and temperatures plummet, sea ice forms on the surface of the Arctic and Southern Oceans. When summer returns, the ice retreats. Winter and summer, expand and retreat—so it has been for thousands of years.

This changing sea ice is vital for life in the oceans. It stops the Arctic and Antarctic coasts being worn away by wind and waves. Predators, such as the polar bear, travel out to sea on the ice for miles during winter, searching for prey. Other animals, such as walruses and penguins, can rest on the ice in between hunts. When the ice melts in summer, nutrients frozen into the sea water are released into the ocean once more, encouraging plankton to grow. Without the ice, these creatures cannot survive.

But now the planet is getting warmer, less of the ocean is freezing in winter, and the sea ice that remains is melting faster than before. Without the white ice to reflect the sun's rays away from the poles, the oceans are getting even warmer, meaning even less sea is cold enough to freeze. The thinning and loss of sea ice is affecting the climate all over the Earth. This change will make a big difference to life in our oceans.

Protecting Our Oceans

Atlantic Ocean
Size: 32,870,000 square
miles (85,133,000 sq km)

Pacific Ocean
Size: 65,144,000 square miles
(168,723,000 sq km)

Dear Reader,

wl grew up by the North Sea with its crashing winter storms and sparkling blue waves in summer. Later, I went to live on an island in the warm, turquoise Indian Ocean. I've watched the Atlantic surf breaking and listened to the roar of the Pacific Ocean. The sea has always fascinated me with its ever-changing colors and sounds and the wealth of life within it.

Most of our planet is made up of the ocean, but it is in trouble. With the climate warming, we're losing the sea ice in the Arctic and Southern Oceans. This affects a host of wildlife and is making the climate warmer still. The warmer sea water elsewhere is killing off coral reefs and all the living things that make their homes there. Plastic discarded by humans is drifting out to sea and killing animals, while pollution is contaminating the oceans. The plants and algae in the ocean have

Arctic Ocean
Size: 5,427,000 square miles
(14,056,000 sq km)

Indian Ocean
Size: 27,243,000 square miles
(70,560,000 sq km)

Southern Ocean
Size: 7,849,000 square miles
(20,330,000 sq km)

always worked hard to supply the planet with oxygen and absorb carbon, but that job is becoming harder.

Every living thing on the planet needs the oceans, including us. Together we need to raise awareness about the problems the oceans face, and protect the creatures that live there. If we stop using and throwing away single-use plastic, we can reduce the amount of trash floating in the ocean.

Humans must be careful not to overfish to protect life in the seas. We can reduce global warming by reducing the amount of energy we use and by switching to sustainable energy. Many people are working hard to find ways we can all care for our planet. I hope this book will inspire you to find out what more you can do to help the oceans, so they can remain wonderful havens of life and beauty that we can all enjoy.

Charlotte Guillain

Index

Find Out More

Books

Knowledge Encyclopedia Ocean! (DK Children)

Discover the Ocean Layer by Layer by Julia Adams (Arcturus Publishing)

How It Works: Oceans by Stephen Hall (Award Publications Ltd)

Ocean Atlas by Tom Jackson and Ana Djordjevic (White Lion Publishing)

The Coral Kingdom by Laura Knowles and Jennie Webber (words & pictures)

Websites

Visit the National Geographic website for kids to find out more about oceans and the animals that live in them: www.natgeokids.com/uk/discover/geography/general-geography/ocean-facts/

Learn about the diversity of wildlife in the oceans and the problems that they face on the WWF website: www.worldwildlife.org/habitats/ocean-habitat

Discover more facts about the oceans and the life in them on the National Ocean Service website: oceanservice.noaa.gov/welcome.html

You can learn more facts and see pictures of mangroves, corals, and many ocean creatures around the world on this website: ocean.si.edu